CW01272104

DISCOVERING WATER

Contents
Water for Life 2
Salty – or Fresh? 8
Fresh Water 14
Drinking Water 19
Glossary 23
Index 24

written by
Angela Lucas

designed and illustrated by
Susannah Bradley

YOUNG LIBRARY

First published in 1992 by
Young Library Ltd
3 The Old Brushworks
56 Pickwick Road
Corsham, Wiltshire SN13 9BX
England

© Copyright 1992 Young Library Ltd
All rights reserved

ISBN 1 85429 012 6

Printed in Hong Kong

Water for Life

Do you say 'How amazing!' when water flows from a tap that you have turned on? Of course not. Hot and cold running water is something most of us take for granted. We drink water every time we are thirsty. We also drink it in tea, coffee, and cool drinks. We use some in cooking. We run plenty when we take a bath or shower. It disappears down our sinks and through our washing machines. About a bucketful (9 LITRES/2 gallons) goes down the toilet every time we flush it. We turn the hose on to wash the car or water the garden. People who live where there is plenty of water use about fifteen bucketfuls (130 litres/28 gallons) every day.

Most of us get water easily, by turning a tap. For some people it is harder work. This Mexican woman draws up water from a well because there is no piped water in her village.

Schools, shops, and hospitals use water too. Huge quantities are needed in factories. Can you guess how much is used in making one car? 100,000 litres/22,000 gallons. Farms use lots too. Every cow drinks about eighty times more than you do every day.

Even we are made of water – about 70 per cent of our body is water. It is not just slopping about inside us. Skin, muscles, blood, brains, and every other part of us are partly water. The brain you are thinking with now is 85 per cent water!

Although water is part of us, it does not all stay inside us. We lose about one litre/0.2 gallons a day when we go to the toilet. We lose more by sweating. We even lose some as we breathe out, and speak.

That does not mean we spray water out of our noses and mouths, but when we see little clouds leaving our mouths on frosty days we know we are losing water.

Your body has to take in as much water as it loses. A thirsty feeling lets you know that your body is short of water. If you could not have a drink, quite soon you would become ill; and after several days without, you would die.

This bar chart shows that humans are 70 per cent water. It also shows the proportion of water in some of the foods we eat.

You do not have to drink every drop of water you need. You eat water as well! Animals and plants contain a lot of water, so when you eat meat, fruit, or vegetables, you take in water. Meat is about 70 PER CENT water. A slice of bread does not taste very wet, but about 35 per cent of it is water. What about a tomato? It is 95 per cent water. No wonder it is juicy.

Every living thing needs water. We can see that animals drink, but what about plants? They do not have mouths, so how do they drink? Their roots draw up water from the soil. It rises up their stems into the leaves, where it helps to make plant food.

The sun shines on the leaves, warming them, and they transpire (breathe out) rather like people do.

Only a few plants can store water. Most have to keep taking it in. When you see plants withering in dry weather it is time to get the watering can.

So now we know that animals, plants, and people all need water. Where does this water come from?

Salty – or Fresh?

There is plenty of water in the sea. Three-quarters of Earth is under the sea. About 97 per cent of Earth's water is sea water. But what was it like when you got some in your mouth? SALT! It is no good for drinking, then.

Of course, we use the seas in other ways. Tankers and container ships carry cargoes across them. Trawlers fish in them. We sail, swim, and scuba-dive at the seaside. But when we want a drink we look for FRESH WATER.

Where is this little 3 per cent of fresh water? About 2 per cent is frozen into ICE at the north and south poles. So all the animals, plants, and people on earth rely on just 1 per cent of its water.

You can see some of this water in rivers and lakes, and falling as rain. The rest is hidden in the earth. All this adds up to just that 1 per cent of all Earth's water. Yet look at what we do with it — we pour much of it away! If 'down the drain' meant 'gone

Here are two uses of water — one for salt, one for fresh. On the left, men are irrigating cotton fields in Kangwane, in the Transvaal. On the right is a tidal power station in Nova Scotia.

for good' all life on Earth would soon wither away. Luckily for us it does not mean this.

In fact, water is never gone for good. We cannot destroy water. To understand this we need to know what it is made of. In one way you can see for yourself. It is a liquid (that is, it flows). It has no colour. It is transparent. A chemist would say it is H^2O – that is his way of saying what it is made of. H stands for hydrogen. O stands for oxygen. Each of these is

Snow is formed of partly frozen vapour in the clouds. Steam is water which has been heated until it boils.

made of tiny parts called atoms. When two atoms of hydrogen and one atom of oxygen come together, they make a molecule of water.

How much is a molecule? A molecule is slightly bigger than an atom, but it takes millions to make one drop of water.

H^2O is not always running water. When it is cold enough it changes to ice. When it is heated enough it changes to STEAM. We see water become ice in the freezer. We see water become steam when we boil a kettle. The little clouds leaving our mouths on frosty days are H²O in the form of VAPOUR (tiny drops so light that they float in the air).

If you cool steam, or heat ice, they will turn back into water. When cold vapour warms up, or warm vapour cools down, they turn back into water also.

The only way to destroy water is to split the hydrogen atoms from the oxygen atoms and never let them get together again. Scientists can do this with a very tiny quantity, so tiny it hardly counts.

When a lot of snow falls, it blocks the roads. The snow plough has to come to clear it away.

Icebergs are huge blocks of ice broken from glaciers. They drift in the sea until they melt.

But when the hydrogen and oxygen come together again, they are water once more.

When we let water go down the drain we have not got rid of it. It joins up with lots of other water. In the next chapter we will see what happens to it.

13

water droplets fall as rain

wind blows water droplets across land

Fresh Water

rain flows into rivers and out to sea

Fresh water comes from rain. What makes rain? The sun shines on the seas, rivers, and lakes. It warms the water and changes some of it into vapour. The vapour rises into the air. High up, it cools. Cooling vapour forms into clouds. Winds blow the clouds across the land. When they cool

rising vapour cools into water droplets

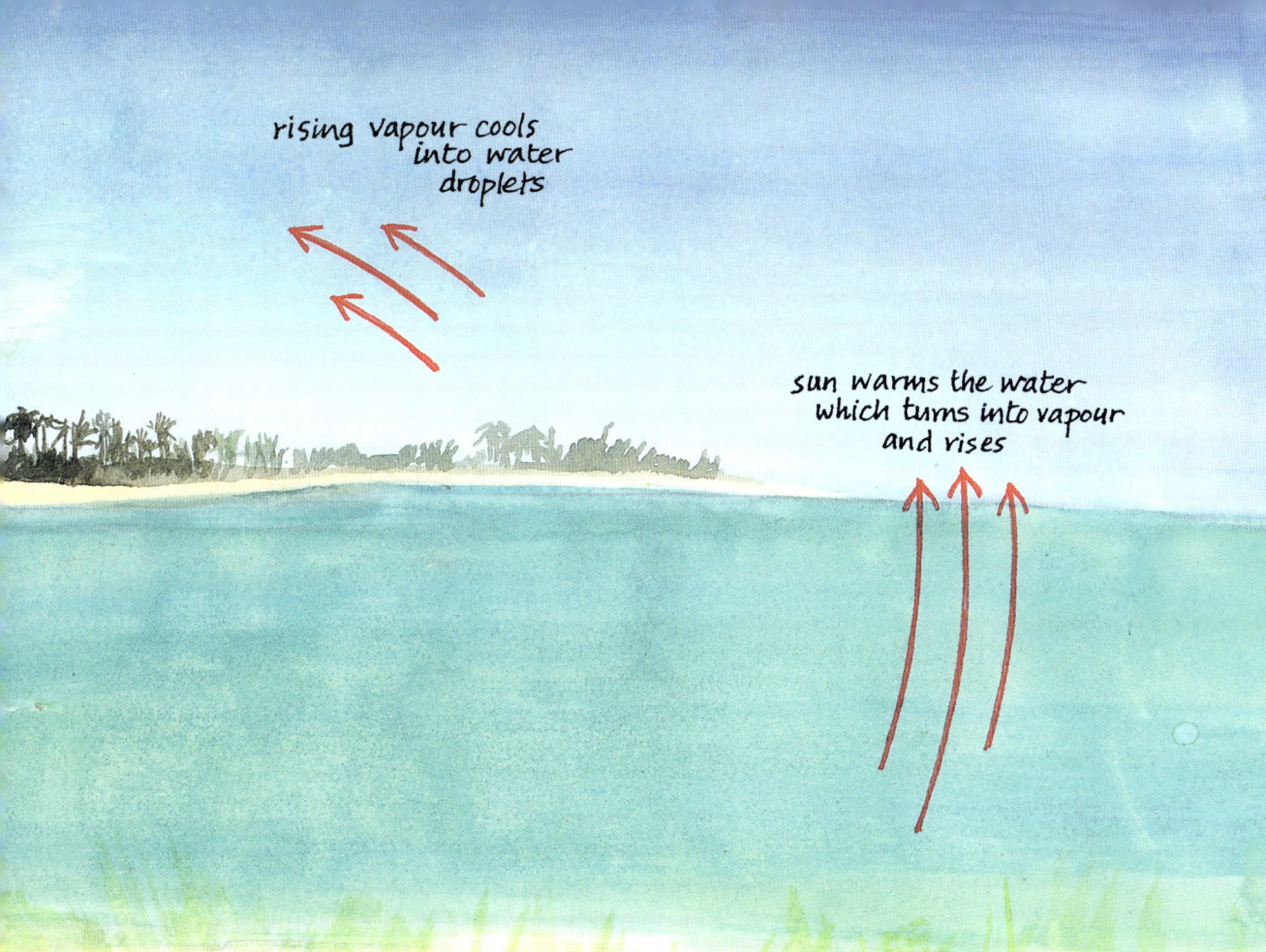

sun warms the water which turns into vapour and rises

enough they become large drops of water, and fall as rain, or – where it is very cold – as snow.

We call this movement of water 'the water cycle'. The sun heats the water, up goes the vapour, and down comes rain or snow.

Rain does not fall evenly all over the earth. In

some lands there is little or no rainfall each year. This causes a DROUGHT, and the drought causes a famine – a desperate shortage of food. There are other places where it rains so much that the people build their houses on stilts over the swamps, and go about in boats.

Many of us live where there is usually a good mixture of wet and dry weather. We have enough

After a year without rain the land is too dry to support life. This cow has died of thirst.

water, but not too much. Even here, though, we sometimes have a long spell of hot, dry weather. We use a lot of water and the level in the lakes and rivers drops very low. Then we are asked to save water, and told not to use a hose. There is still the same amount of water in the world, but it has gone somewhere else, and we cannot get at it.

Now and again the opposite happens. We have a tremendous downpour of rain. It goes on for so long that rivers and lakes overflow, flooding fields, roads, and houses. People have to be rescued. There is plenty of water about, but it is too dirty to drink.

This chapter is all about 'fresh' water. So why are we saying it may be 'dirty'. The reason is that 'fresh' doesn't always mean 'clean' – it means 'not salty'. Fresh water may be POLLUTED, therefore not clean enough to drink. We must never drink water straight from a river or lake. We would risk becoming very ill if we did.

River water has mud and leaves in it, and often much nastier things too. When farmers use chemicals on their crops, these can drain from the fields into the rivers. Factories use chemicals, too, which get washed out into the drains and from there into the rivers. The dirty water from our toilets is piped away from our houses to the SEWAGE WORKS. There it is cleaned up a bit, and put back into the river, but it is not yet clean enough to drink.

All this 'fresh' water must be thoroughly cleaned before it is safe to drink. In the next chapter we see how this is done.

Drinking Water

Water that flows from our taps has to be very pure indeed. Where does it come from? Some of it comes from rivers. The water company builds a DAM across the river to hold the water back. More and more river water builds up against the dam. Eventually a lake is formed. Lakes formed in this way to store water are called RESERVOIRS. The

This dam was built across a South African river. Look at the height of the lake which has built up behind the dam.

reservoir

dam

strainer

filter

gravel and sand

more chemicals

pumping station

water is stored there until it is needed.

When the water is to be used, it is taken from the reservoir along underground pipes to a TREATMENT WORKS. Here it is treated to make it perfectly clean. Safe chemicals are added to kill germs. Then the clean water is stored in a service reservoir. The service reservoir is covered to keep the water clean.

underground reservoir

pumping station

aeration tank

chemicals

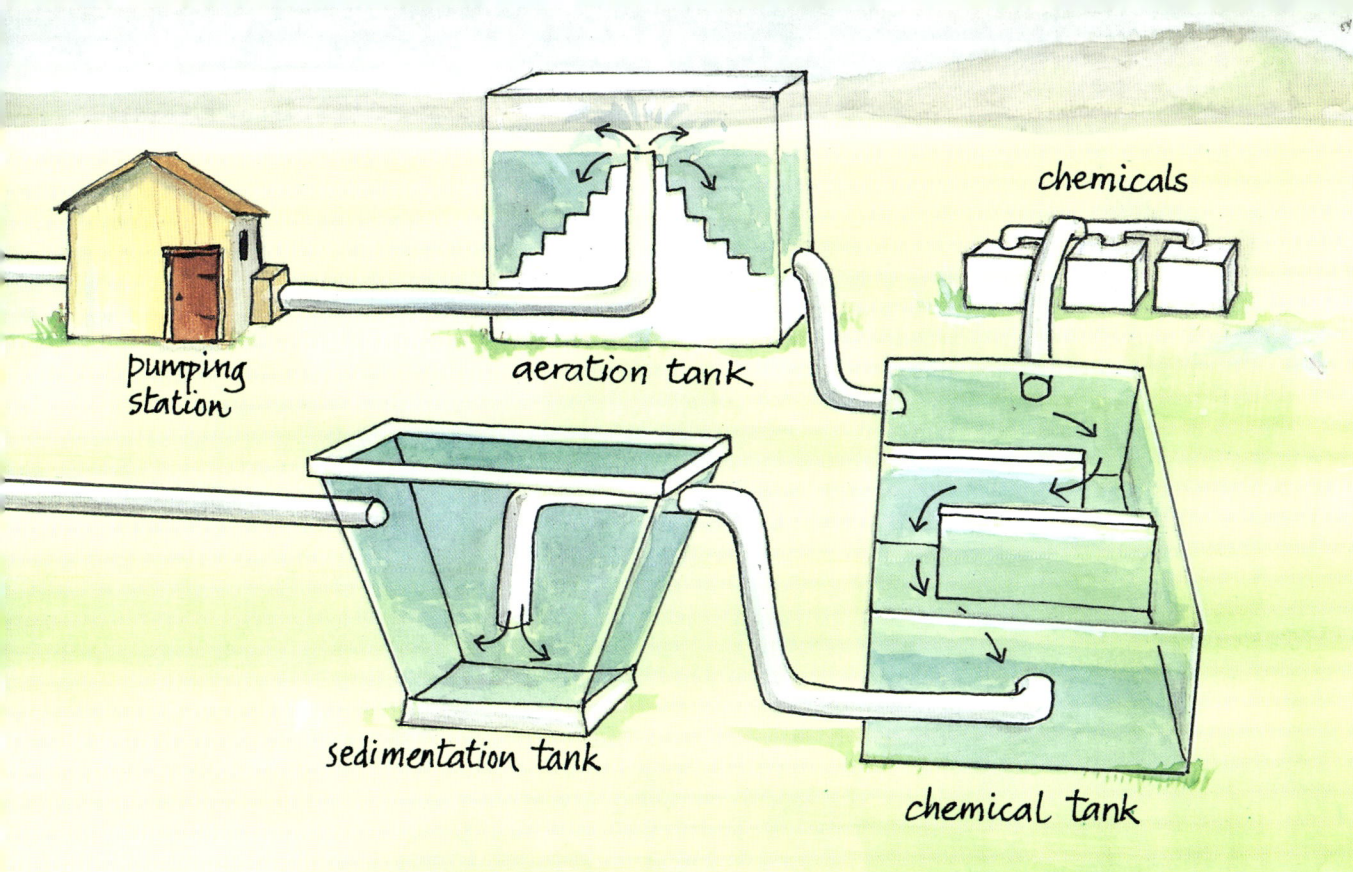

sedimentation tank

chemical tank

Water companies also take water from AQUIFERS. Aquifers are stores of underground water which form naturally. They are not underground lakes. They are very large areas of rock which is full of tiny holes. Water seeps into the holes and is held there. It cannot drain away because rock without holes is underneath.

Geologists find this water by studying the rocks near the surface, and the plants which grow there. Then engineers bore down into the aquifer and pump up the water. This water is called ground water. It is much cleaner than river water. It needs

AQUIFER

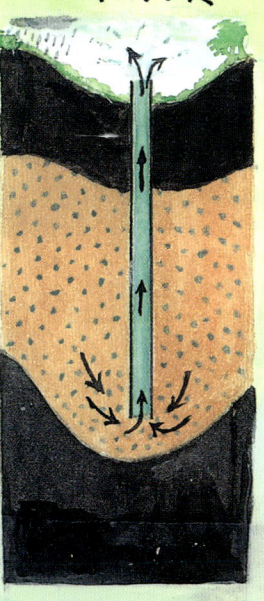

Non-porous rock:
Porous rock:

only a little treatment before it is stored in the SERVICE RESERVOIR.

Clean water is sent along underground pipes to homes, schools, factories, hospitals, and all the other places we need it. The water companies have to keep checking that the water they supply is perfectly clean. Small amounts of unwanted chemicals could remain in the water even after treatment. Farmers are told to be careful with the chemicals they use. Factory owners are made to treat used water before they let it go back into the rivers.

All of us can help to look after our rivers. Watch for rubbish building up, or streaks of oil on the surface. Dead fish floating on the surface are a sign of serious pollution. Things like this should be reported at once. Perhaps in your school you could keep a river watch as a class project. You can get advice on this from National Rivers Authority. Their address is in your local phone book.

Glossary

aquifer: An area of underground rock which holds water.

dam: A wall built across a river to hold the water back.

drought: A long period without rain.

fresh water: Water which is not salty (but it might be unfit to drink for other reasons).

ice: Water which has frozen and turned solid.

litre: A metric measure equal to 1.7 pints.

per cent: A portion of 100. For example, 4 per cent means 4 hundredths.

polluted: Polluted water is water unfit to drink because of other things added to it.

reservoir: A lake (natural or artificial) used to collect and store water.

salt water: Water which is too salty to drink. All sea water is salty, and so are various large lakes in very hot, dry countries.

service reservoir: A lake in which clean, treated water is stored.

sewage works: The place where waste water is cleaned sufficiently to return it to a river.

steam: Water which has boiled, and turned into vapour.

treatment works: The place where fresh water is made clean and fit to drink.

vapour: Drops of water so small and light that they drift in the air.

Photo Sources

Australian Tourist Commission, London: page 16.
Canadian Embassy, London: pages 9 (left), 10 (left), 13 (right), cover and page 1 (bottom centre).
Environmental Picture Library: pages 3, 13 (left).
New Zealand Tourism: page 10 (right).
South African Embassy, London: pages 9 (right), 19.
Young Library: cover and page 1 (top left and middle right)

Index

aquifer 21, 23

dam 19, 23
drought 16, 23

floods 17
fresh water 8, 14, 18, 23

glaciers 13
ground water 21

ice 8, 11–12, 23

Mexico 3

National Rivers
authority 22
Nova Scotia 9

pollution 18, 22, 23

rain 14–17
reservoirs 19–20, 22, 23
rivers and lakes 9, 14, 17, 18

salt water 8, 9, 23
service reservoir 22, 23
sewage works 18, 23
snow 13, 15
steam 11–12

transpiration 7
Transvaal 9
treatment works 20

vapour 12, 14

water: in animals 4–7
in plants 6–7
pollution 8, 22, 23
properties of 10
salty 8, 9, 23
uses of 2–4, 8
water cycle 15
water companies 19–22

Artwork
Among the subjects illustrated are the water cycle, pages 14/15; stilted houses in Borneo, pages 16/17; a helicopter spraying pesticide, page 18; a beaver building its dam, page 19; a water treatment plant, pages 20/21; and a school river watch project, pages 22/23.